IGFA's 101 Freshwater
Fishing Tips and Tricks

K.T. MAE

Other Books by Bill Dance

Practical Black Bass Fishing (with Mark Sosin)

There He Is (The Art of Plastic Worm Fishing)

Techniques on Bass Fishing

Bass N' Objects

Bill Dance on Crappie

Bill Dance on Largemouth Bass

IGFA's 101 Freshwater Fishing Tips and Tricks

Bill Dance
Illustrations by Rod Walinchus

Skyhorse Publishing

Skyhorse Publishing books may be purchased in bulk at special discounts for
sales promotion, corporate gifts, fund-raising, or educational purposes. Special
editions can also be created to specifications. For details, contact the Special
Sales Department, Skyhorse Publishing, 307 West 36th Street, 11th Floor, New
York, NY 10018 or info@skyhorsepublishing.com.

Skyhorse® and Skyhorse Publishing® are registered trademarks of Skyhorse
Publishing, Inc.®, a Delaware corporation.

Visit our website at www.skyhorsepublishing.com.

10 9 8 7 6 5 4 3

Library of Congress Cataloging-in-Publication Data
Dance, Bill.
IGFA's 101 freshwater fishing tips and tricks / Bill Dance ;
illustrations by Rod Walinchus.
p. cm.
ISBN-13: 978-1-60239-000-3 (pbk. : alk. paper)
ISBN-10: 1-60239-000-2 (pbk. : alk. paper)
1. Fly fishing–Miscellanea. I. International Game FishAssociation. II. Title. III.
Title: 101 freshwater fishing tips andtricks. IV. Title: One hundred one freshwater
fishing tips andtricks.
SH456.D23 2007
799.1'1–dc222006102589

Printed in the United States of America

IGFA's 101 Freshwater Fishing Tips and Tricks

1

When Texas rigging or Carolina rigging soft plastic baits like worms, lizards, tubes, or other creature lures in a weedless configuration, always keep your bait straight with the hook and line to prevent line twist and eventual hang ups.

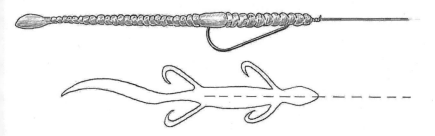

Keep your bait straight.

2

Always match your hook size to the head diameter of the soft plastic bait you're using. Example: On an 8-inch plastic worm use either a size 4/0 or 5/0 hook: On a 4-inch worm a size 1/0 to 2/0 hook.

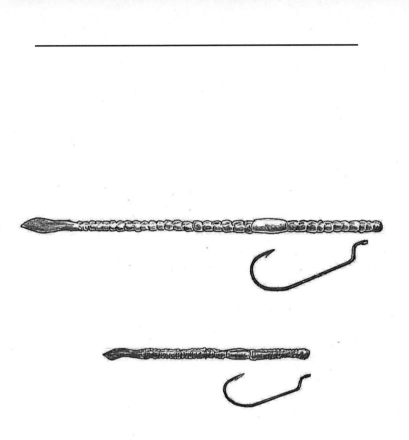

Match hook size to bait.

3

When fishing summertime bass in a small body of water such as farm ponds or soil conservation and natural lakes, remember that in the heat of summer most mini-waters lack enough oxygen down below. Bass rely on the shallows where there is a small, narrow, oxygen-rich band of water. Most anglers fish below the bass, in low-oxygen areas, mistakenly thinking summertime bass ought to always be deep.

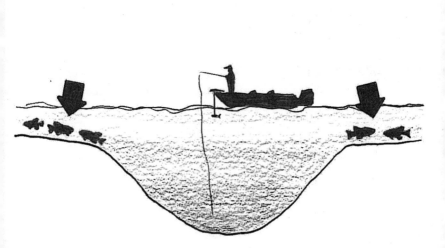

Go shallow for summertime bass.

4

Normally, dark-colored lures work best during low-light conditions such as early and late, on cloudy days, and in stained-to-muddy water.

5

When fishing muddy or off-colored water, fish shallow, fish objects, fish slow, and make repeated casts.

Fish shallow structure slowly in muddy water

6

During the cold winter months the key to success is to fish *clear* water with *slow* presentation-type lures, especially when water temps are in the mid-to-low 40 degree range.

7

When fishing murky or muddy conditions, use lures that vibrate. Dark-colored, bulky, shallow-running crankbaits or single, Colorado-blade spinnerbaits are good choices.

Vibrating lures for murky conditions

8

Shallow timber and brush that is close to deep water will generally hold more bass. In visible timber, begin looking for fish in deep pockets on brush- or timber-covered flats, around isolated patches, and along distinct tree or brush lines. Points, pockets, and bends along the edges are better than straight portions.

Brush near dropoffs holds promise.

9

Research has shown that mature bass show a decided preference for crawfish and, contrary to popular belief, the lowly crawfish is the most prevalent forage in our lakes, ponds, sloughs, creeks, and rivers. There are good reasons for the preference. Bass feeding on crawfish grow much faster than those who live where crawfish are not abundant. Crawfish also are much easier to catch, therefore bass expend less energy to gain the high-protein nourishment that crawfish provide.

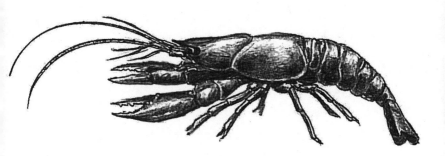

Crawfish create big bass.

10

Bluffs that are stair-stepped under the water are especially productive because they offer bass a choice of depths. Find a bluff that's close to a deeper channel and usually you've hit paydirt.

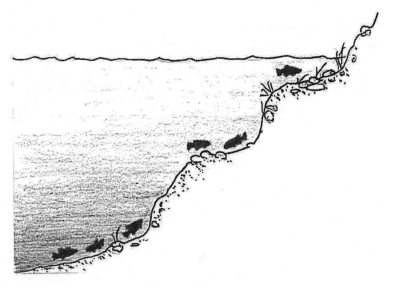

Stepped bluffs offer bass a choice.

To gain the quickest depth with a crankbait, use one with a straight lip.

Straight-lip crankbaits dive fastest.

12

When bass are reluctant to bite, a tactic that works extremely well is to fish slowly with smaller lures. The idea is to make it as easy as possible for the fish to take your offering with minimum effort.

13

One popular way to guess the weight of a bass when you have no scale is to multiply the length x length x girth and divide by 1,250. This will provide a fairly good estimate of the fish's weight. With spawning fish full of roe and with exceptionally fat fish, this rule will not be as accurate.

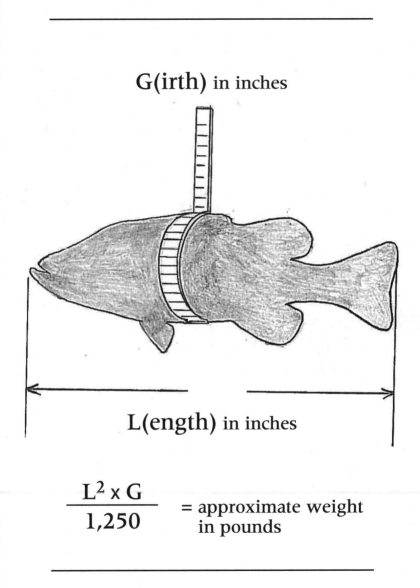

G(irth) in inches

L(ength) in inches

$$\frac{L^2 \times G}{1,250} = \text{approximate weight in pounds}$$

14

When shoreline fishing gets tough, make an about face. Why? Lakes change, fish change, and anglers must change as well. From the bass's point of view the advantages of open water are strong and numerous: Less pressure, more forage, better habitat as a rule, and there's more comfort in the way of oxygen, safety, and temperature.

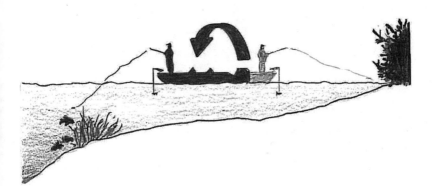

Don't neglect open water.

15

When reeling or fighting a bass on a baitcasting reel, it's best to palm or cup the reel's side plate with your left hand. It creates better sensitivity, more power when fighting a fish, and doesn't tire your wrist like holding the rod handle.

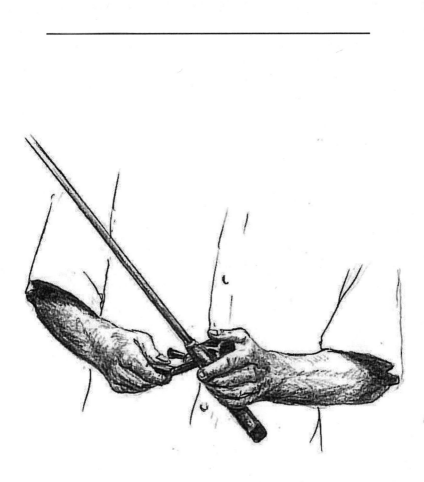

Palming provides power and control.

16

When bass fishing familiar waters in your area, don't get hung up on the same old spots. Spend some time looking for new spots and locations you've never tried before, with some lures you might not ordinarily use. You'll probably be surprised at the results!

17

It's important to remember that fish feed heavily by sight in clear water, but in stained water, vision begins to lose its primary importance and fish use a mixture of sight, smell, and sound to locate their prey. In muddy water fish rely mostly on sound and smell.

18

Always avoid bending or pulling your rod back past the point at which the grip and the line create a 90 degree angle. Over-stressing the rod can break 18 to 24 inches off the tip regardless of how well it's made.

Overstressing snaps rodtips.

19

"Establishing a rhythm" with a topwater lure attracts bass. How you retrieve the bait determines the rhythm and can make a tremendous difference in your success or failure.

20

Two of the most important elements to consider in crankbait fishing are depth and speed. Also, color, shape, and size should be always be carefully matched to existing conditions.

21

When fishing around such things as old boat docks or bridge pilings, some fishermen make the mistake of casting directly into the walls at right angles instead of making parallel casts, so it takes several casts to do what one should do. Always take the time to position your boat for parallel casts and your lure will be in the strike zone longer. Drop your lure well past where you think the fish are—spots of shade, for example—and then retrieve it alongside the available structure.

Parallel casts keep lure in the strike zone.

22

Taking springtime water surface temperatures is important because it gives you a starting point to consider, but bottom and mid-range temps are much more important, especially in shallow depths.

23

Here's a tip to remember when crankbait fishing: Water temperatures can affect depth. The warmer it gets, the thinner the water becomes. The colder water gets, the thicker or denser it becomes. Obviously then, a crankbait will dive a little deeper in thinner or warmer water. In many situations, an extra foot or two can really make a difference.

24

When trying to gain more depth with a crankbait, it's important to consider line size and diameter, lip position, body profile and shape, distance of cast, retrieve speed, type of material the lure is made of, and finally, whether it's a floater or suspender.

25

Never pass up fishing a boat-launch ramp. Most are made of concrete, stretch way out into the lake, and slope downward, thereby making a clear pathway from deeper to shallower water. Normally on a ramp you'll find rip-rap rock stretching out along the edge of the concrete into deeper water. Algae will grow on these hard rough surfaces during the late spring, summer, and early fall months. This attracts some of the bass' favorite food—shad, minnows and small bluegill—to feed on the algae. Bass then follow to feed on these baitfish.

Look for fish at launch ramps.

26

A stump or a treetop, by itself, might hold a fish or two and so can a submerged point extending out toward deeper water. But a stump or treetop sitting right smack in the middle of this same point can really be a smokehouse! This is what we call multiple structure—a good fish holding spot located right on top of another.

Stay alert for multiple structures.

27

Surely some lures work better than others and catch more fish, but it is common to find one bass specialist who swears by a certain bait and an equally competent angler who complains that he can't catch a fish on it. The size, weight, and color of a lure can make all the difference and so can the manner in which it is presented to the fish. Always remember that the biggest single factor in artificial lure fishing is *confidence*. If you don't honestly believe it will catch fish, you're probably wasting your time using it.

28

There are times when every one of your lures will probably work, but most of the time only a handful of them will do the job well. It's a mistake for fishermen, especially beginners, to jam-pack a tacklebox with a multitude of different baits. A much better approach is to select a few basic types that can cover all depth ranges and learn to fish them with perfection. A good mix would include spinnerbaits, plastic grubs, worms and eels, vibrating-type crankbaits, and a few topwater lures. This can be modified more closely to suit the waters fished most often.

29

Wash fish you plan to eat in clean water and put them on ice as soon as possible. Fresh fish have little odor, but unless they're put on ice immediately, enzymes and bacteria break down tissue and the "fishy" smell develops.

30

To fishermen, a "deadhead" is a fallen tree that has floated for some time. At some point one end of it has become waterlogged and either sunk to the bottom or hung up on a ledge or other submerged cover. Any deadhead is an excellent place to locate bass, but a deadhead that is wedged along a drop-off to deeper water is always better. Never pass these up! Single bass will hang out around the exposed end near the surface and concentrations of fish often hold in the thick cover below.

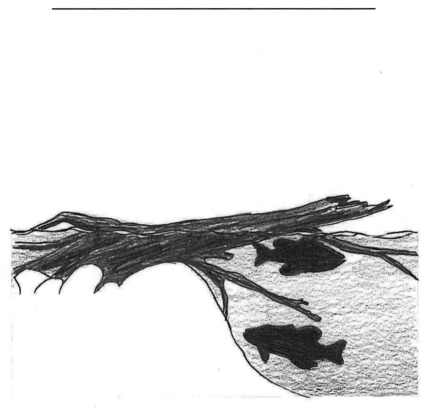

Deadheads gather fish.

31

Two of the most important controls a fisherman has at his disposal are depth control and speed control. This is especially true with crankbaits. If the lure is not worked at the fish's depth level, he may not hit it unless he's extremely active, so getting the lure down to his depth level is just as important as making an accurate cast to him. Once the lure is down, always remember that your retrieve—whether fast or slow—should be erratic. The key word here is "control."

Keep the lure in the strike zone.

32

Seventy-five percent of all line failure occurs at the knot. Be sure to tie a good one and check it often for fraying or nicks. Retie frequently.

Check knots often for fraying.

33

As predators, bass exhibit a number of general tendencies. Two of the most important ones involve how they feed in a school of baitfish. Contrary to the belief of some fishermen, a bass does not merely open its mouth and crash through a school of shad in a random manner. In order to feed effectively, a fish must isolate a specific victim and then pursue it. At the same time, a fish is more prone to select a prey that appears disabled or one that looks different in some way from the others. This is why it's so important to create an erratic action with your lure on the retrieve.

Bass seek out unusual action.

34

What makes one dock or pier better than others? Two key things: cover and deep water! Any dock with planted cover and deep water close by is definitely a great place to fish. Watch for piers that have lights and pole holders on them, because this can be your tip-off to planted cover below. Such piers are usually owned by an angler who has placed treetops or artificial attractors around them to attract gamefish.

Look for docks with habitat improvements.

35

It's important to select a lure that'll work at a depth the fish are using. And, it's important to pick one that has a proper shape, size, and color to look somewhat natural in the particular body of water where you plan to use it. If you are going for big bass, for example, a blue, 8-inch plastic worm is often a good choice, but if the lake you plan to fish just happens to be muddy, it would not be nearly as effective as, say, a chartreuse-and-black spinnerbait. Why? First, because the worm would create very little sound—it's more of an eye-contact lure for use in clearer water. And second, blue is a better color choice for clearer water.

Choose lure type carefully.

36

Falling water, whether natural or induced, can sometimes really be puzzling to a fisherman regardless of what fish is being pursued. A drop of an inch or so usually doesn't affect fish, but a foot or more can. If the drop is great enough to leave most of the cover in a lake exposed, it can make fishing really tough. But by closely observing the cover that is exposed and making some careful notes, you can turn this disappointing time into a real bonanza later on, when the water rises again.

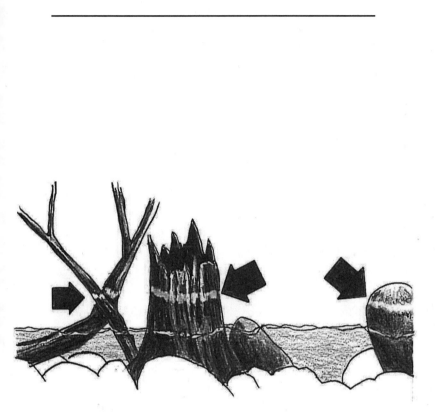

Take notes when water levels drop.

37

When you're trying to catch bass in the wind, a few changes in tactics can make all the difference. First, cut back on the size of your line and increase the size of your weight. This will serve several purposes. It will allow you to gain depth quicker when you're using lures like a jig-n-trailer, a slip sinker worm, a grub, or a Carolina rig. The longer you must wait for your lure to sink, the more your boat will drift under poor control. Seconds can make the difference in success or failure. The smaller diameter line and heavier weight will also help eliminate those dreaded backlashes, which can be much more prevalent on windy days.

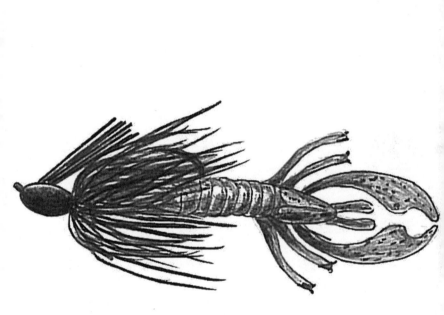

Light line and big baits beat windy days.

38

One trick to landing bigger fish is to get control of the fish quickly—before it knows what happened! Get him headed toward you and keep him headed toward you! Countless fish are lost because they are allowed to position themselves with their powerful tail sweeping them away from the angler. Keep in mind the old saying *"Where the head of the fish goes, the tail must follow."*

Keep 'em coming!

39

For effective flippin,' there are two important considerations: lure presentation and boat placement. You have to put your lure *exactly* on target with as little commotion as possible. Allowing your lure to splash into the water will void the technique, as will making noise in your boat.

40

In simple terms, *structure* refers to the irregular features of a lake bottom that differentiate it from the surrounding bottom. A stump tipped on its side in a foot or two of water along the shoreline is structure and a creek bed meandering its way along the lake bottom in twenty-five feet of water is also structure. Because fish often feed along structure and use it as a secure place to hide, the reason it's important to fishermen should be obvious. Find the right structure, you'll usually find the fish!

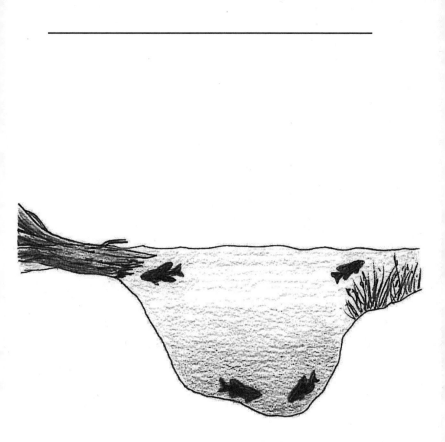

"Structure" means any irregular feature.

41

Most people work a plastic worm way too fast. This comes from getting used to the faster pace of crankbaits or buzzbaits to cover a lot of water. With rare exception, the name of the worm game is "slow, slow, slow" and you just have to keep reminding yourself to slow it down and fish it methodically. Many fishermen also sweep a worm too far, because they use the rod. Always use wrist action instead of arm motion—this will work the worm in short hops.

Slow down with worms.

42

All aquatic creatures make noises that fish can hear and predator fish are often attracted and triggered to strike by these sounds. Fishermen should always keep in mind that the sound an artificial lure makes can be just as important as how good the lure looks, especially in off-colored water.

43

Confidence can't be bought in a sporting goods store or acquired from another angler. It's something that must be earned, primarily through experience. You'll never learn everything there is to know about fishing, but by continuing to learn and experiment, you will acquire confidence in what you are doing. By developing an understanding of the habits and habitat of your quarry, by mastering the intricacies of your equipment, and by slowly putting together the pieces of the fishing jigsaw puzzle, you'll become extremely confident. Then you'll see why confidence is the most important lure in your tacklebox.

44

You'll pick up a lot of bass that other fishermen miss if you make it a point to cast to areas with marginal shade. I've seen bass hiding behind one thin stick-up that provided only enough shade to cover one of their eyes, but apparently it still made them feel comfortable and secure. I've also seen bass use each other for shade.

Minimal shade can hold bass.

45

Are bigger bass really smarter? Even a little 12-inch bass has to be gifted with special senses and instincts to reach his size, so consider how very gifted bigger bass, say those over six pounds, must be. They say you don't get old being a fool. So it goes with fish. The big guys really have to be smarter—just to survive.

46

Many times, you can look at a body of water and get some idea of how good a place it is to fish just by noting the wildlife. The next time fishing gets slow, look around the shoreline and try to spot squirrels moving in the trees, or listen for birds singing. Chances are you won't see or hear much of anything. What's happening above the water with wildlife can be a real clue to what's happening below.

47

Rising water doesn't present nearly the bass fishing challenge to me as falling water. When lake levels drop, bass begin to lose their habitat—when lake levels rise, their habitat is expanded. This is a time to look for new, rich areas where fish will move to feed. I usually begin by finding water about a foot or two deep that has flooded a very large area. Large schools of shad will often move into these areas searching for plankton—one of their favorite foods. And naturally, the bass will follow the shad to feed on them. Watch carefully for baitfish activity on the surface. During the warmer months, when water temperatures are above 70 degrees, a buzzbait can be fantastic in such situations. If the water is murky, a spinnerbait might be the best offering.

Rising water levels expands habitat.

48

Barometric pressure affects all living creatures. When the pressure changes rapidly, whether it's rising or falling, fishing also changes, and sometimes drastically. Bass can start feeding in a frenzy when a storm front approaches and this is usually indicated by fast-falling pressure. The exact opposite usually occurs when the pressure starts back up—it's almost impossible to get fish to hit until the barometer gets back to normal. When the mercury is on the rise, I usually direct my attention to bass in deeper water, or at least to fish that have quick access to deeper water. They simply aren't affected as much by pressure changes as bass in shallow water.

When bass are not in a chasing mood, slow down and offer them a slow presentation-type lure like a plastic worm, lizard, tube, grub, or light weight jig-and-plastic combination.

50

When considering water clarity, how clear is clear? Well, here's an easy gauge to go by. Under sunny conditions, if knowledgeable anglers can see a light-colored lure in depths of four feet or more, they call that clear water. If they can only see the lure down two to four feet, they call that stained; and if they can only see the lure down two feet or less, it's muddy.

Use your lure to gauge water clarity.

51

All things considered, a spinnerbait is probably the top producer among bass lures. This is not to imply that other lures don't work, because each of them have its place in certain situations. But spinnerbaits are one of the most versatile. You don't miss many strikes on them and they can be configured with different blade sizes and shapes to fish everywhere from shallow to deep. You can fish them in open water or in some really tough cover, in clear water to muddy, day or night and at most times of the year. They're perfect for adding trailers and you can buzz them just under the surface or fish them at a snail's pace. And finally, they allow you to cover a lot of water very quickly.

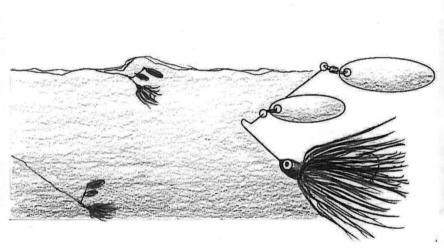

Spinnerbaits offer versatility.

52

On virtually all lakes, points can be among the best places to fish—that's why you hear pro fishermen say "points point out bass." With few exceptions, points offer one key characteristic that makes them attractive to fish—there's almost always a depth change nearby and that will make the fish stay in the vicinity! It's best to look for points that extend way out into a lake and then drop abruptly. Study topo maps carefully and be sure to use a good graph or flasher unit to determine the depth where fish are holding. Then when you locate the drop-off, mark it well with marker buoys, being careful to not spook the fish.

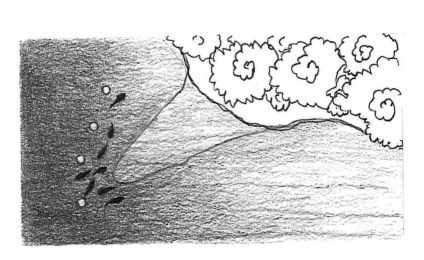

Use topo maps to locate structure.

53

When fishing for post-frontal bass, it's best to fish early and late in the day when sun penetration of the water is minimal. Confine your fishing to deeper areas adjacent to known productive shallower areas and remember these two key words: FISH SLOWLY! Yes, catching bass during this period is tough, but patience, determination and work can pay off handsomely.

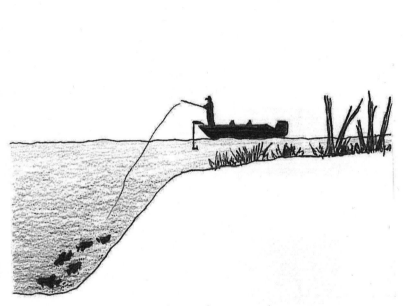

Bass go deep as fronts move in.

54

Suspended bass hang out in open water some-where off the bottom and while it's true that they don't hit as readily, they can be caught. For this type of fishing, rely heavily on your flasher or LCG to locate the fish, then concentrate on those that are shallower than say fifteen feet, simply because they will be easier to work. Jigging spoons or deep crankbaits often work great in such situations and don't be afraid to experiment.

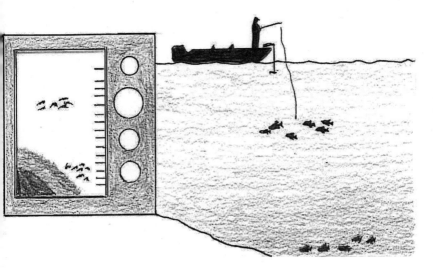

Electronics pinpoint suspended bass.

55

Catching any kind of fish on artificial offerings requires the use of what I call the "three rights." Put the "right lure" in the "right place" with the "right retrieve" and you're well on your way to catching more fish than the angler who doesn't consider the three rights every time he makes a cast. Of course, you're not going to be successful every time regardless of what you do, but you'll be "right" more often than not with the "three rights."

56

Spinnerbaits are one of the most versatile fishing lures you can use. When fishing a spinnerbait deep, I recommend using a single-blade bait. You have better feel for the blade rotation and it vibrates better than dual-blade baits. Be sure to experiment with different blade combinations, sizes, and colors to find what works best under a given set of circumstances.

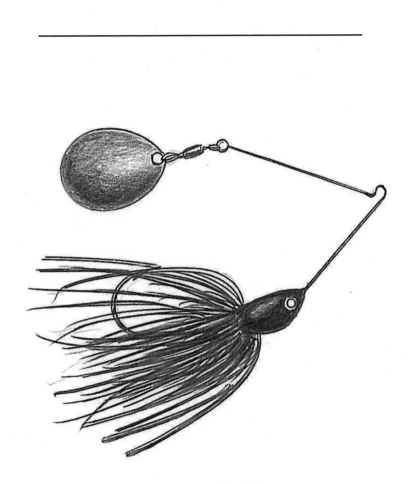

Single-blades work depths best.

57

Did you know that most trophy bass are females? Scientists have proven that the female-to-male ratio becomes weighted in favor of females after the age of five years. In most of the lakes tested, studies have shown a ratio of one female to four males in the first year, changing to one female to just two males in the second year. By age six, the ratio drops dramatically to six females to *no* males, so chances are any trophy you land will be a female!

58

One of the biggest mistakes topwater fisherman make is to fail to let the fish get a good hold on the lure before they set the hook. This is understandable, because nothing is more exciting than seeing bass explode on a topwater offering. Train yourself to wait before you set the hook. A good rule is to set the hook only after the lure has vanished from sight and you "feel" the fish.

Give 'em time to grab it!

59

It's important to make sure that all your lures have sharp hooks, but it's especially critical with top-water lures. Sharp hooks give you a slight edge if the fish happens to strike slightly off center or not as solidly as you would hope for. Also, except with buzzbaits, allowing a little slack in your line slows your reaction time and makes most topwaters work better.

Slight slack helps with topwater hookups.

60

Casting is a learned routine and anyone can perfect their accuracy by doing one thing—practice, practice, practice. Remember the old saying "practice makes perfect?" The best time to improve your accuracy is when you're on dry land—not while you're fishing. If you wait until you're out on the lake, you'll waste a lot of precious time. Set aside a few minutes each day to practice in your back yard and always select a specific target. Then, try to put your lure on the mark every time. An old bicycle tire makes a good medium-sized target. Later on you can graduate to something smaller, like an empty coffee can.

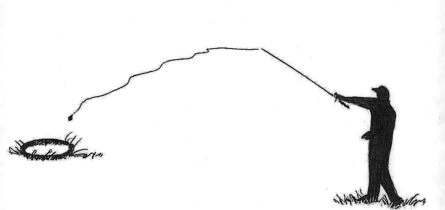

Practice in the yard, not on the water.

61

The single most important factor in fishing is finding the correct depth. If you're not fishing the correct depth, you're wasting time. The finest angler around can fish the best bait in the world, but if he's fishing it at the wrong depth, he won't do very well. Fishing at the correct depth, almost anyone can catch a few fish.

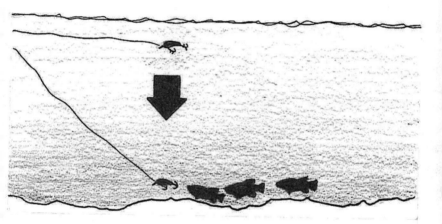

Correct depth is key to success.

62

Underwater springs are typical in watersheds and these are places you should always fish. The area near the spring will be cooler in summer and warmer in winter, because the spring temperature will remain more constant. Not knowing a spring is present can cost you fish.

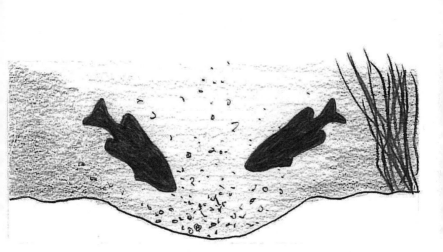

Be alert for springs.

63

When fishing, it's important to be observant. Often you can spot schools of baitfish by an oil slick on the surface, because baitfish leave a natural discharge. If the school is moving quickly, the slick will appear upwind. Obviously, if the school is milling around in one area, wind currents will push the slick below them. Polarized fishing glasses can be a big help here, too. Baitfish will show up as dark areas below the surface. Also, watch for single baitfish breaking the surface.

Learn to spot baitfish schools.

64

In early spring when water surface temperatures reach the mid- to high 50s, start looking for shallow spawning pockets—areas protected from the wind with maximum exposure to the sun. Here, try spinnerbaits with blade sizes and colors that suit the prevailing water clarity. In clear water, for example, white baits with white blades can be a good choice.

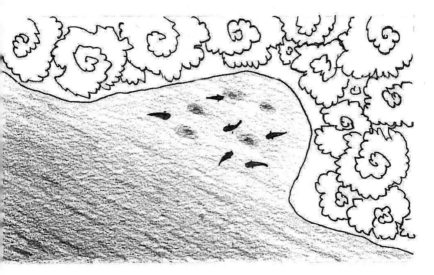

Shallows warm fastest in springtime.

65

One of the favorite springtime spawning structures for smallmouth bass is an inundated flat, so-called because of its low gradient from the shoreline to deeper water. But the type of flat that you'll find most productive is somewhat different than that preferred by largemouths. They like flats loaded with cover like logs, brush or grass, but smallmouths like flats with only sparse, scattered cover.

Smallmouths like sparse cover.

66

Long, tapering points with bottoms of clay and gravel are great smallmouth spawning grounds. Some bigger females prefer points over other areas because they provide quicker access to deeper water. Look for isolated patches of weeds or stumps. You'll probably find nests a few feet from these, instead of right next to them.

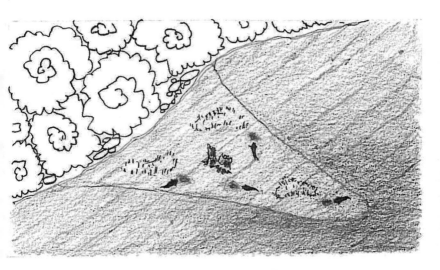

Points provide prime spawning for smallmouths.

67

Don't hold spawning female fish in your livewell so you can carry them back to the dock to show off to your buddies. If you do, you can forget about those fish returning to their nests when you eventually release them. Instead, bring along your camera, shoot a quick picture right after the fish is caught, then let it go quickly. Believe me—watching them swim away is a great feeling!

68

Using Carolina-rigged worms will allow you to cover a larger area when you are trying to find staging bass just before the spawning season. When bass are getting ready to go on nests, they migrate to nearby staging areas like points and flats.

Prospect pre-spawners with Carolina jig.

69

Generally speaking, the color of the water will usually be the biggest factor in determining which color lure the fish will go for. Start by trying brighter fluorescent colors in stained water, and natural colors when it's clear.

70

When the water rises, bass move shallower; when it falls, they move deeper. Fluctuations will affect bass in shallow water more, and a rapid change will have a more drastic effect on fish movements than a gradual change.

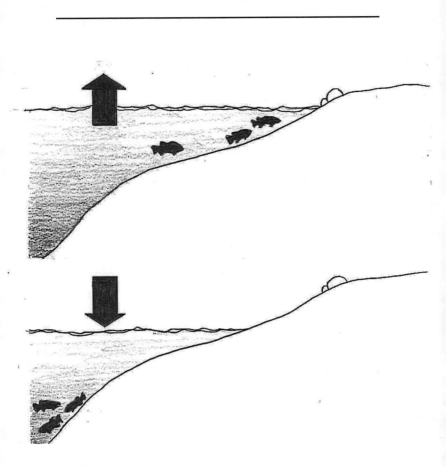

Falling water drives bass deep. Rising water brings them up.

71

A common error that you should avoid when fishing farm ponds is consistently fish only the shallows when the bigger fish have moved to deeper water. Try fishing whatever deep structure is there, perhaps a channel ledge, submerged mound, or deep point and you'll probably connect with the bigger fish. You may also want to place artificial fish attractors at strategic locations for different seasons of the year.

Remember to prospect deep structure.

72

During early spring migrations, crappie usually feed heavily, building up energy for the upcoming spawn. During this period, they are fairly easy to catch, once located, *and* provided you offer them something they can see and relate to. Remember that crappie use sight almost 100 percent in their selection of food, so choose your baits and colors wisely.

73

Be careful to match your line size to your lure when topwater fishing. If your line is too heavy, it won't impart the action it should to topwater lures. Ten-pound-test is one of my favorites.

74

Never pass up casting at likely looking stumps, and in lakes where the water level fluctuates drastically, take the time to mark them so they can be found easily during high water. During low water stages, drive long bamboo canes or sections of PVC pipe into the ground beside the stumps. When the water rises again, the markers remain visible above the water line.

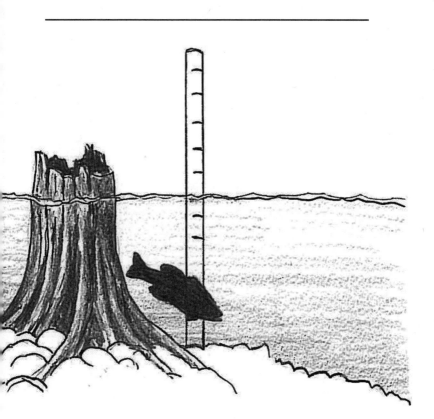

Features marked during low water pay off during high water.

75

Small isolated patches of grass will often produce more fish than large areas. Find one of these close to deep water and it can really make your day. In areas where the grass does not fully reach the surface, a well placed topwater lure can draw the fish from great distances.

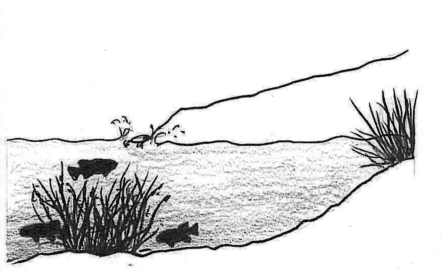

Isolated, submerged grass often holds fish.

76

Quality regulations, part of which entail slot limits requiring the immediate release of all fish falling into particular size groups, are vitally important to restoring good fishing where it no longer exists. Please obey them and recognize that this is a small price to pay and a worthwhile investment to preserve a great natural resource.

77

In small streams, bass will rarely hold in fast currents, so look for slack water below obstructions. Eddies, undercut banks, log jams, and deep pools with still water are all likely holding areas. A fallen tree in a deep pool is always a hotspot that will pay off time and again. Always cast upstream or across the current and then work your lure into the slack water.

Seek out slack areas in moving water.

78

When night fishing, look for shallow shoals adjacent to where you usually find bass during the day and try breaks that lead to deeper water. At first, try dark colored lures like topwaters or shallow runners that create a lot of vibration or noise to attract the attention of the most active feeders. Next, switch to deeper runners or big plastic worms and fish even deeper.

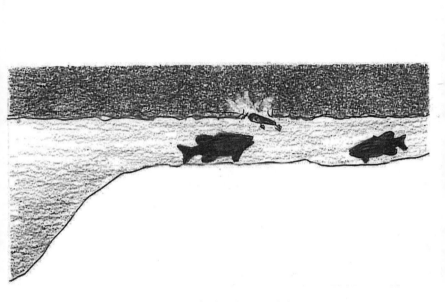

Use noise and vibration at night.

79

In bluff-walled lakes, rock slides often carry trees and brush into the water. These may provide the only cover available in these areas, so they're always worth a few casts.

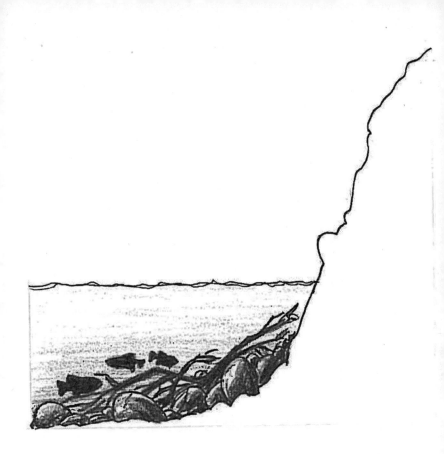

Submerged bluffs accumulate cover and structure.

80

The most popular knot among anglers, when using monofilament line in pound tests below 30, is a reverse clinch.

Use reverse clinch in lines lighter than 30-pound.

81

Cold water is denser than warm water, therefore it's reasonable to assume that your bait can achieve greater depths in 80 degree water than it can in 60 degree water. This 20 degrees of difference may allow your bait to reach another foot or so of depth, and at times, this can determine whether or not you catch fish!

82

On the larger reservoirs, some of the best places that I've found to fish for large crappie, later in the year after they spawn, are around and under bridges. Bridge pilings provide plenty of shade from the burning sun and there are usually plenty of minnows around them.

Bridge pilings and crappie are a natural combination.

83

Nighttime can be a great time for summer crappie fishing. Lanterns or specialty floating lights hanging on or near your boat will attract bugs of every variety. Crappie in large numbers will readily rise to feed on the minnows that are feeding on the bugs attracted to the light.

Light draws bugs; bugs draw minnows;
minnows draw crappie.

84

As with most species of fish, you have to alter your tactics somewhat for good catches of bluegill when the weather is really hot. At times, bridge pilings and boat docks can offer some action, but weedlines next to deep water and deeper water structure will usually hold a better grade of fish. Weedlines are good because they offer three very important requirements of the fish: cover, food, and dissolved oxygen.

Weedbeds hold the better bluegill.

85

Natural-lake bass seldom have as much structure and cover to choose from as those in the larger reservoirs, so it's not uncommon for them to suspend out in open water. This is especially true during the summer and winter months.

In lakes lacking cover, seek suspended fish.

86

Deep water forms distinct layers in summer. The coolest layer is on the bottom, but it usually lacks oxygen making it uninhabitable for bass. The middle layer, called the *thermocline* is a zone where the temperature changes rapidly, and the top layer is an area of warmer water. Bass usually stay above the thermocline, but will move into it if the upper layer becomes too hot.

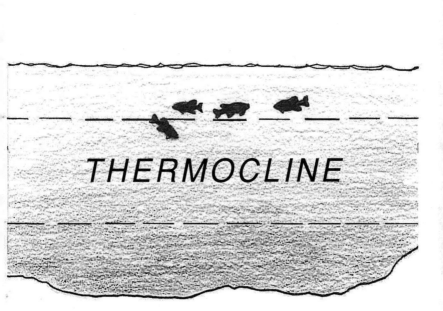

Look for bass above the thermocline

87

Some good places to look for bass in reservoirs during the summer months are: Points long the main channel; deeper sections of submerged creek channels; bends along the main river channels; riprap on an embankment; along stair-stepped bluffs; and in feeding areas such as brushy flats.

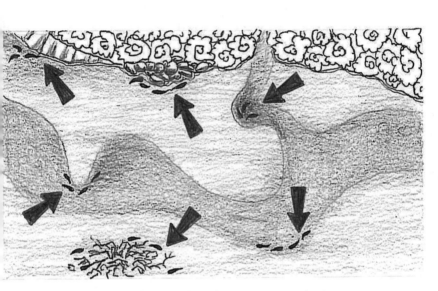

Hunt the drops and depths in summer and winter.

88

Schools of summer crappie are often found around any wooden structure along deep water ledges and drop-offs, and this pattern is good through early September. They will hold in areas that are similar to their winter hangouts, but will be considerably shallower, say 12 to 30 feet. The clear water typical in summer dictates using light line—2- to 8-pound test—and small, 1/16-ounce to 1/32-ounce jigs.

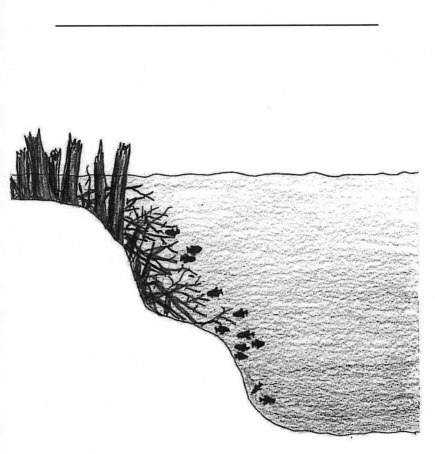

Clear conditions call for light lines and small jigs.

You should gauge the lure size you use for crappie by the average grade of fish you're catching. In areas where there are plenty of big crappie, they'll hit a good-sized lure, because they're usually feeding on the larger shad. Smaller fish require a smaller bait.

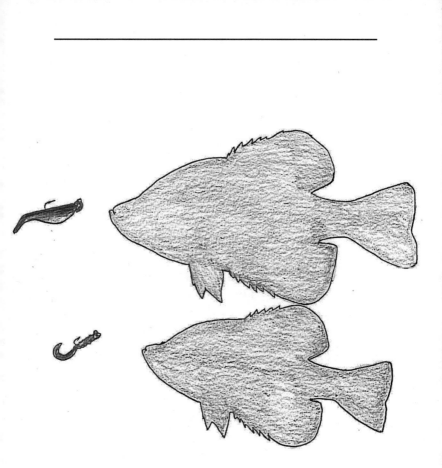

For bigger crappie, fish larger lures.

90

Generally speaking, the best largemouth streams will have slow to moderate current and warm water. The best streams for smallmouth will have cooler, clearer water. Excellent holding spots for both species include eddies, deeper pools, undercut banks and gravel bars.

Gravel bars and points offer cover in moving water.

91

Some bluegill will bed throughout the year. Active bedding periods for summer bluegills are usually signaled by full moon phases. About three to five days before a full moon, male bluegills will be actively guarding nests. Watch for them in the same general areas where spring spawning took place— just don't expect to find as many nests.

Watch the moon for bedding bluegill action.

92

It's not cooler water, but shade that draws fish to boat docks and similar cover when the sun is bearing down. If you doubt this, check the water temperature just below the surface and you'll notice that it's about the same in the shade as it is in sunlight. The simple rule of diffusion causes this. Significant water temperature changes occur only with depth.

Shade, not temperature, draws fish to docks.

93

Docks that are built closer to the water surface hold more fish, because they provide more shade. Recognize that casting there requires a side-arm presentation to get your lure to "skip" up under the dock. And keep your boat a reasonable distance away to avoid spooking the fish.

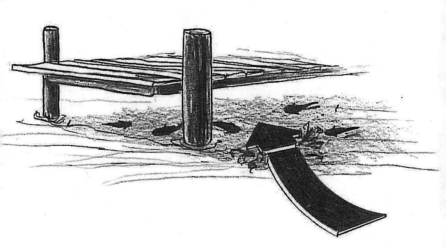

Hang back and skip baits under low docks.

94

Here's the best way to set your reel drag: First thread your monofilament through the rod guides. Then have a buddy pull on the line while you flex the rod and apply tension just as you would in a real fishing situation. Adjust the drag until the line can be stripped without breaking when you rare back with the rod as if setting the hook on a fish. Watch the tip of your rod. If it bends too far down before the drag begins to slip, or bounces erratically when the drag is working, your reel probably needs a good cleaning.

Smooth drags mean fewer fish lost.

95

To make an exact replica of any fish, all a good taxidermist needs is the length and girth measurements and a good color photo of your catch. Replicas usually look better than actual fish, and because the modern materials used are far superior to the fish's skin, such mounts last much longer.

96

Because winds travel in a counter-clockwise direction around low-pressure areas, fishermen can use them to locate the nearest storm. Face into the wind, raise your right arm out parallel to the ground and to the right, and you will be aiming at the approximate center of the closest low pressure area, and probably the nearest storm.

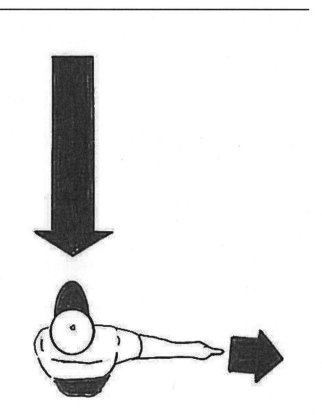

Face the wind, point right. There's the storm.

97

Fishing for bluegills is best on warm, sunny days with little wind and it's not uncommon for the fish to bite all day long. While a simple bobber rig baited with crickets has enticed many a bluegill, small ½₂-ounce jigs cast on ultra-lite tackle offer lots of action. For me, black is the best color jig, and I use 4-pound-test line.

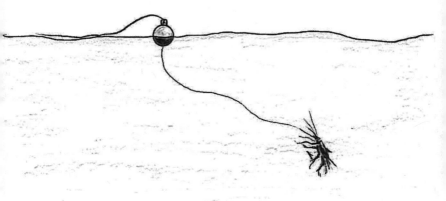

Cricket-and-bobber is a proven bluegill getter.

<u>98</u>

After spawning, smaller bluegills usually remain in shallow water in the weeds, but the bigger ones move deeper. Look for them along deep edges or drop-offs near lily pads or other vegetation, and they can be as deep as 12 to 18 feet. Any group of pads can hold a few fish, but the best ones will have an irregular edge and be near deeper water.

Bigger post-spawn bluegill go deep.

99

Matching the color of your lure to the clarity of the water and prevailing light penetration can often mean the difference in success or failure. Chrome-colored lures, for example, often closely match what bass expect to see in bright, clear water. Regardless, the best bet is to experiment with different colors. Sometimes they'll attack one color ravenously while totally ignoring another.

100

Crappie and weeds just go together naturally and some of the best places to target your search are the outside edges of visible weedlines, and any irregular features along the grassline drop. These features include cuts, ditches, canals, channels, depressions, pockets, or points. Of course, you may sporadically pick up a few fish anywhere, but you'll save valuable fishing time by concentrating on these higher-percentage areas.

Weedlines are winners for crappie.

101

A rapid rise or fall in water level has a much greater impact on fish movement than a gradual change and it takes longer for water levels to change in lakes or reservoirs than it does in rivers and streams. When possible, plan your fishing trips accordingly.